The
Choise of Valentines

Or

THE MERIE BALLAD OF

NASH HIS DILDO

By

THOMAS NASH

Edited by

JOHN S. FARMER

Copyright © 2013 Read Books Ltd.
This book is copyright and may not be
reproduced or copied in any way without
the express permission of the publisher in writing

British Library Cataloguing-in-Publication Data
A catalogue record for this book is available from the
British Library

Thomas Nashe

Thomas Nashe is considered to be one of the greatest of the English Elizabethan pamphleteers. He was also a playwright, poet and satirist. Nashe was the son of Parson William Nashe and Margaret (née Witchingham), born in 1567 and baptised in November of that year. He was one of seven children and spent his early life at Lowestoft, Suffolk, England. Nashe was lucky however, as, alongside his brother Israel, he was one of the only two children to survive infancy. In 1573, the family moved to West Harling, near Thetford after Nashe's father was awarded a position at the Church of All Saints.

Around 1581, Thomas Nashe went up to St John's College, Cambridge as a sizar, gaining his bachelor's degree in 1586. He left Cambridge two years later, in 1588. After gaining this education, Nashe then moved to London and started his literary career in earnest. The remaining decade of his life was dominated by two concerns: finding an adequate patron and participating in controversies, most famously with Richard and **Gabriel Harvey**. Nashe's first appearance in print was his preface to **Robert Greene**'s *Menaphon*, which offers a brief definition of art and overview of contemporary literature. After this (and the publication of *Anatomy*) he was drawn into the **Martin** Marprelate controversy (resulting from several anonymous tracts that attacked the **episcopacy** of the **Anglican Church**). Nashe was on the side of the bishops. As with the other writers in the controversy, his share is difficult to determine. He was formerly credited with the three '**Pasquill**' tracts of 1589–1590, which were included in **R. B. McKerrow**'s standard edition of Nashe's works, however McKerrow himself later strongly argued against Nashe's authorship.

In contrast to these religious and political concerns, Nashe also took on more 'earthly' subjects. Sometime in the early 1590s, he produced an erotic poem, *The Choice of Valentines* that begins with a sonnet to 'Lord S'. It has been suggested that *The Choice of Valentines* was written possibly for the private circle of **Ferdinando Stanley, 5th Earl of Derby** (then known as Lord Strange). It has alternatively been suggested that 'Lord S' refers to the Earl of Southampton, Shakespeare's patron. It describes the Valentine's Day visit of a young man named 'Tomalin' to the brothel where his lover, 'Mistris Francis', has recently become employed. Tomalin poses as a customer and having paid ten gold pieces for her favours, Tomalin makes his way towards his erotic goal. As can be imagined, the text caused quite a stir!

Nashe's friendship with Robert Greene (the author of *Menaphon*, for which Nashe provided the preface) drew Nashe into the Harvey controversy, involving the brothers Richard and **Gabriel Harvey**. In 1590, Richard Harvey's *The Lamb of God* complained of the anti-Martinist pamphleteers in general, including a side-swipe at the *Menaphon* preface. Two years later, Greene's *A Quip for an Upstart Courtier* contained a passage on 'rope makers' that clearly refers to the Harveys (whose father made ropes). The passage, which was removed from subsequent editions, may have been Nashe's. After Gabriel Harvey mocked Greene's death in *Four Letters*, Nashe wrote *Strange News* (1593). Nashe attempted to apologise in the preface to *Christ's Tears Over Jerusalem* (1593), but the appearance of *Pierce's Supererogation* shortly after offended Nashe anew. He replied with *Have with You to Saffron-Walden* (1596), with a possibly sardonic dedication to **Richard Lichfield**, a barber of Cambridge. Harvey did not publish a reply, but Lichfield answered in a tract called 'The Trimming of Thomas Nash' (1597). This pamphlet also contained a crude woodcut portrait of Nashe, shown as a man disreputably dressed and in **fetters**.

Alongside this running dispute, Nashe produced his more famous works. While staying in the household of Archbishop **John Whitgift** at **Croydon** in October 1592, he wrote an entertainment called *Summer's Last Will and Testament*, a 'show' with some resemblance to a **masque**. In brief, the plot describes the death of Summer, who, feeling himself to be dying, reviews the performance of his former servants and eventually passes the crown on to Autumn. The play was published in 1600. Nashe is widely remembered for three short poems, all drawn from this play and frequently reprinted in anthologies of Elizabethan verse: 'Adieu, farewell, earth's bliss,' 'Fair summer droops' and 'Autumn hath all the summer's fruitful treasure.' Moving on from this success, in 1597 Nashe co-wrote the play *The Isle of Dogs* with Ben

Jonson. The work caused a major controversy for its 'seditious' content and was quickly supressed, never to be published.

The chronology of Nashe's last days is uncertain. He was alive in 1599, when his last known work, *Nashes Lenten Stuffe*, was published, and dead by 1601, when he was memorialised in a Latin verse in *Affaniae* by **Charles Fitzgeoffrey**. A recent book has provided linguistic and other evidence to support a theory that Thomas Nashe re-entered London as 'Thomas Dekke'' after he was banished from the city in the summer of 1597 (after *The Isle of Dogs* debacle). It proposes that he faked his death and permanently assumed the Thomas Dekker identity after the Archbishop of Canterbury burned Nashe's books and banned him from all future publishing in mid-1599. This theory is highly controversial though, and Nashe – the eminent controversialist, remains a mystery.

INTRODUCTION.

Nash's "CHOISE OF VALENTINES" has apparently come down to us only in manuscript form. It is extremely doubtful (Oldys notwithstanding[a]), whether the poem was ever before accorded the dignity of print. Nor would it now be deemed worthy of such were the only considerations those of literary merit or intrinsic value: truth to tell there is little of either to recommend it. But, as it has been repeatedly said, and well insisted on, the world cannot afford to lose any "document" whatsoever which bears, or *may* bear, in the slightest degree, on the story of its own growth and development, and out of which its true life has to be written. Especially is even the meanest Elizabethan of importance and value in relation to the re-construction—still far from complete—of the life and times of the immortal bard of Avon. In the most unlikely quarters a quarry may yet be found from which the social historian may obtain a valuable sidelight on manners and customs, the philologist a new lection or gloss, or the antiquary a solution to some, as yet, unsolved problem.

The Choise of Valentines - Or the Merie Ballad of Nash His Dildo

"The Choise of Valentines" claims attention, and is of value principally on two grounds, either of which, it is held, should amply justify the more permanent preservation[page viii] now accorded this otherwise insignificant production. In the first place, it appears to have been dedicated to the Earl of Southampton, the generous patron of letters, and friend of Shakspeare; and second, it is probably the only example extant of the kind of hackwork to which Nash was frequently reduced by "the keenest pangs of poverty."[b] He confesses he was often obliged "to pen unedifying toys for gentlemen." When Harvey denounced him for "emulating Aretino's licentiousness" he admitted that poverty had occasionally forced him to prostitute his pen "in hope of gain" by penning "amorous Villanellos and Quipasses for newfangled galiards and newer Fantisticos." In fact, he seems rarely to have known what it was to be otherwise than the subject of distress and need. As an example of these "unedifying toys" the present poem may, without much doubt, be cited, and an instance in penning which his "hope of gain" was realised.

It is a matter of history that Nash sought, and succeeded in obtaining for a time, the patronage of the Earl of Southampton, one of the most liberal men of his day, and a prominent figure in the declining years of Elizabeth. "I once tasted," Nash writes in 1593,[c] "the full spring of the Earl's liberality." Record is also made of a visit paid by him to Lord Southampton and Sir George

Carey, while the former was Governor, and the latter Captain-General, of the Isle of Wight.

From internal evidence it would seem that this poem was called forth by the Earl's bounty to its author. "My[page ix] muse devorst from deeper (the *Rawl. MS.* reads *deepest*) care, presents thee with a wanton elegie;" and further on, the dedication promises "better lines" which should "ere long" be penned in "honour" of his noble patron. This promise is renewed in the epilogue:—

"My mynde once purg'd of such lascivious witt,

With purifide words and hallowed verse,

Thy praises in large volumes shall rehearse,

That better maie thy grauer view befitt."

Does this refer to "The Unfortunate Traveller; or, The Life of Jack Wilton," generally regarded as Nash's most ambitious work, and which he dedicated to Lord Southampton in 1593? If so, and there is no evidence to gainsay the conclusion, we can fix the date of the present poem as, at all events, prior to 17th September of that year, when "The Unfortunate Traveller" was entered on the Stationers' Register.[d] This would make Nash contemporaneous, if not prior to, Shakspeare in offering a tribute to the merits of the young patron (Southampton at that time was barely twenty years old) of the Muses. *Venus and Adonis* was entered on the

Register of the Stationers' Company about five months earlier, on the[page x] 18th April, 1593, and barely more than two months prior to the registration of "The Terrors of the Night."

It is curious to note that while Shakspeare and Nash both promise "graver work" and "better lines," they alike select amatory themes for their first offerings. The promise in Shakspeare's case was redeemed by the dedication to Southampton of "The Rape of Lucreece," while it may be assumed, as aforesaid, that Nash followed suit with "The Unfortunate Traveller."

Nash, however, for some cause or other failed to retain the Earl's interest; "indeed," says Mr. Sidney Lee, "he did not retain the favour of any patron long." It is only fair to state, however, that the withdrawal of Lord Southampton's patronage may not have been due to any fault or shortcoming on the part of Nash, for there is likewise no evidence whatever to show that any close intimacy existed between Southampton and Shakspeare after 1594. Probably there was much else to claim Lord Southampton's attention—his marriage, and the Essex rebellion to wit. This, however, leads somewhat wide of the present work.

So much for the circumstances which appear to have called forth "The Choise of Valentines." The next consideration is, Has it ever appeared in print before? Oldys, in his MS. notes to Langbaine's *English Dramatic Poets* (*c.* 1738) says:—"Tom Nash certainly wrote and published a pamphlet upon Dildos. He is accused of it by his antagonist, Harvey." But he was writing nearly 150 years after the event, and it is certainly very strange that a production which it can be shown was well known[page xi] should, if printed, have so entirely disappeared. At all events, no copy is at present known to exist.[e] John Davies of Hereford alludes to it, but leaves it uncertain whether its destruction occurred in MS. or in print. In his "Papers Complaint"[f] he writes:—

But O! my soule is vext to thinke how euill

It is abus'd to beare suits to the Deuill.

Pierse-Pennilesse (a *Pies* eat such a patch)

Made me (agree) that business once dispatch.

And having made me vndergo the shame,

Abusde me further, in the Deuills name:

And made [me] *Dildo* (dampned Dildo) beare,

Till good men's hate did me in peeces teare.

As regards the manuscript copies there are one or two points worthy of note. At present we know of two, more or less incomplete, but each of which supplements, in some degree, the other. These MSS. are respectively in

The Choise of Valentines - Or the Merie Ballad of Nash His Dildo

the Bodleian (Rawl. MS. Poet, 216) and the Inner Temple (Petyt MS. 538, vol. 43, p. viii., 295b.) libraries. Both texts are obviously corrupt, the Rawlinson abominably so. Probably the former was written out from memory alone, while the Petyt, if not a transcript direct from the original is, at any rate, very near to it.

The Bodleian version is written on paper in a small oblong leather-covered book, originally with clasps. The penmanship is early 17th century, probably about 1610-20. It is thus catalogued:— ..."*E libris* Matt.[page xii] Postlethwayt, Aug. 1, 1697. Perhaps (earlier) Henry Price owned the book." The volume contains besides an English transcript of Ovid's "Arte Amandis" and some amatory poems.[g] The date of the Petyt text may be about.... It is written in a miscellaneous, folio, commonplace-book, and in the catalogue it is described as "an obscene poem, entitled 'The Choosing of Valentines,' by Thomas Nash. The first 17 lines are printed at p. lx. of the Preface to vol i. of Mr. Grosart's edition of Nash's works, as if they formed the whole piece."[h]

Nothing is known of Postlethwayt and Price, who at one time owned the Rawlinson copy, that throws light on its source. In the Petyt, however, we get a suppositional explanation of its manifestly purer text. Petyt, subsequent to his call to the Bar, in 1670, was for many years Keeper of the Records in the Tower of London. Now we know that Lord Essex, an intimate friend and connection of the Earl of Southampton, and like Southampton a generous and discerning patron of letters, was for some time in the "free custody" of the Lord Keeper of the Tower. Further, Southampton, who had joined Essex in his rebellion, had been tried and convicted with his friend, and though the Queen spared his life, he was not released from the Tower until the ascension of James I. It is not unlikely, therefore, that a copy of Nash's manuscript made for Lord Essex passed, on the execution[page xiii] of the latter, with other papers and documents, into the official custody of the Lord Keeper, to be subsequently unearthed by his successor, Petyt, who, with a taste for the "curious," had it copied for his own edification. This supposition is further borne out as follows: The particular commonplace book in which this poem occurs has been written by various hands. In the same handwriting as, and immediately preceding "The Choise of Valentines," are two poetical effusions dedicated "To the Earl of Essex," both apparently written when he was in prison and under sentence of death. The other contents of the volume are likewise contemporaneous.

All things considered, then, the Petyt text, although transcribed about fifty years later, has weightier claims to attention than the version in the Rawlinson MSS. I have, therefore, adopted the former as a basis, giving the Rawlinson variations in the form of notes. A few of these are obviously better readings than those of the Petyt text: the reader cannot fail to distinguish these. In the main, however, the Inner Temple version will be found consistent with its particular dedication, whilst the Rawlinson variations appear due to an attempt, signally unsuccessful, to adapt the poem for general use.

For the rest I have faithfully adhered to the original in the basic text, and in the variorum readings, except in one particular. The Rawlinson *MS.* is altogether guiltless of punctuation, while the Petyt copy has been carelessly "stopped" by the scribe: I have therefore given modern punctuation.

J.S.F.

FOOTNOTES

a See page 10.

b *Have with you to Saffron Walden*, iii., 44.

c *Terrors of the Night.*

d It is true that Nash, in his dedication of the "Unfortunate Traveller," speaks of it as his "first offering." This, however, must be taken rather as meaning his first *serious* effort in acknowledgment of his patron's bounty, for in "The Terrors of the Night" (registered on the 30th June, 1593), he somewhat effusively acknowledges his indebtedness to Lord

Southampton:—"Through him my tender wainscot studie doore is delivered from much assault and battrie: through him I looke into, and am looked on in the world: from whence otherwise I were a wretched banished exile. Through him all my good is conueighed vnto me; and to him all my endeavours shall be contributed as to the ocean." Again, as evidence that Nash had addressed himself to Southampton prior to his dedication of "The Unfortunate Traveller," we glean from his promise ("Terrors of the Night") "to embroyder the rich store of his eternal renoune" in "some longer Tractate."

e At the same time it must be stated that the scandal of the controversy between Nash and Harvey became so notorious that in 1599 it was ordered by authority "that all Nashes books and Dr. Harvey's books be taken wheresoever they may be found and that none of the said books be ever printed hereafter" (COOPER, *Athenæ Cant.* ii. 306).

f Davies [Grosart, *Works* (1888) 1-75, lines 64-72.]

g These have been incorporated in "National Ballad and Song" (Section 2, *Merry Songs and Ballads*, Series 1).

h This is not quite correct. The title in the MS. runs "The Choise of Valentines," and Dr. Grosart purports to

The Choise of Valentines - Or the Merie Ballad of Nash His Dildo

give the first eighteen lines, but in transcription he has omitted line 4.

TO THE RIGHT

honorable the Lord S.[a]

Pardon, *sweete flower of Matchles* [1] *poetrie,*

And fairest bud the red rose euer bare [2]*;*

Although my Muse, devorst from deeper care [3]*,*

Presents thee with [4] *a wanton Elegie.*

Ne [5] blame my verse of loose unchastitie

For painting forth the things that hidden are [6],

Since all men acte what I in speache declare, [7].

Onlie induced with varietie [8]

Complants and praises [9] euery one can write,

And passion out their pangu's in statlie rimes [10];

But of loues pleasures none did euer write [11],

That have succeeded in theis latter times [12].

Accept of it, Deare Lord [13], in gentle gree,

And better lynes, ere long [14], shall honor thee.

NOTES

a Henry Wriothesley, the Earl of Southampton, and Baron of Titchfield. The dedication is absent in the Rawlinson text: *cf.* variorum reading in line 13.

1 *Matchles*, machles.

2 *the red rose euer bare*, that euer red rose bare.

3 *devorst from deeper care*, diuert from deepest care. Nash was notoriously impecunious all through his life, and probably reference is here made to some bounty received at the hands of Lord Southampton (*see* Introduction). What patronage meant at times is gleaned from Florio's dedication of *The Worlde of Wordes* in 1598 to the same nobleman. He says:—"In truth I acknowledge an entire debt, not only of my best knowledge, but of all; yea, of more than I know, or care, to your bounteous lordship, in whose pay and patronage I have lived some years.... But, as to me, and many more, the glorious and gracious sunshine of your honour hath infused light and life." Rowe also tells a story of Lord Southampton's munificence to Shakspeare. It is said that he gave the poet £1,000 (equal to £12,000 now-a-days) to complete a special purchase. Whether this story be true or not, it is certain that Lord Southampton was a most liberal patron of letters.

4 *Presents thee with*, Presentes you with.

5 "Ne" = Nor, A.S.; *unchastitie*, inchastitye.

6 *painting*, paynting; *things*, thinges; *hidden are*, hidden be.

7 & 8 In Rawl. MS. these lines are transposed. *Since all men act*, sith most men marke; *speache declare*, speech descrie; *Onlie*, only; *varietie*, varyetye.

9 *Complants and praises euery one*, Complayntes & prayses every man.

10 *passion out*, passion forth; *their pangu's*, there loue; *statlie rimes*, statly rime.

11 *pleasures none*, pleasure non; *euer write*, e're indite.

12 *theis latter times*, this latter time.

13 *Deare Lord*, deare loue. A significant reading in view of the absence of the dedication in the Rawl. MS. "*Accept ... in gentle gree*," to take kindly.

14 *And better lynes ere long*, And better farr, ere long (*see* Introduction).

THE CHOOSING OF VALENTINES. [1]

It was the merie moneth of Februarie,

When yong men, in their iollie roguerie[2],

Rose earelie in the morne fore[3] breake of daie,

To seeke them valentines soe trimme and gaie[4];

With whom they maie consorte in summer sheene[5],

And dance the haidegaies[6] on our toune-greene,

As alas at Easter[7], or at Pentecost,

Perambulate[8] the fields that flourish most;

And goe to som village abbordring[9] neere,

To taste the creame and cakes[10] and such good cheere;

Or[11] see a playe of strange moralitie,

Shewen by Bachelrie of Maningtree[12].

Where to, the contrie franklins[13] flock-meale swarme,

And Jhon and Jone com[14] marching arme in arme.

Euen on the hallowes of that blessed Saint[15]

That doeth true louers[16] with those ioyes acquaint,

I went, poore pilgrime, to my ladies[17] shrine,

To see if she would be my valentine[18];

But woe, alass[19], she was not to be found,

For she was shifted to an upper[20] ground:

Good Justice Dudgeon-haft, and crab-tree face[21],

With bills and staues had scar'd hir[22] from the place;

And now she was compel'd, for Sanctuarie[23],

To flye unto a house of venerie[24].

Thither went I, and bouldlie made enquire[25]

If they had hackneis[26] to lett-out to hire,

And what they crau'd[27], by order of their trade,

To lett one ride a iournie on a iade.

Therwith out stept a foggy three-chinnd dame[29],

That us'd to take yong[30] wenches for to tame,

And ask't[31] me if I ment as I profest,

Or onelie ask't[32] a question but in iest.

"In iest?" quoth I; "that terme it[33] as you will;

I com for game, therefore give me my Jill[34]."

"Why Sir," quoth shee, "if that be your demande[35],

Com, laye me a Gods-pennie[36] in my hand;

For, in our oratorie siccarlie[37],

None enters heere, to doe his nicarie[38],

But he must paye his offertorie[39] first,

The Choise of Valentines - Or the Merie Ballad of Nash His Dildo

And then, perhaps, wee'le[40] ease him of his thirst."

I, hearing hir[41] so ernest for the box,

Gave hir hir[42] due, and she the dore unlocks.

In am I entered:[43] "venus be my speede!

But where's this female[44] that must do this deed"?

By blinde meanders, and by crankled[45] wayes,

Shee leades me onward, (as my Aucthor saies[46]),

Vntill we came within a shadie[47] loft

Where venus bounsing vestalls skirmish[48] oft;

And there shee sett me in a leather chaire[49],

And brought me forth, of prettie Trulls[50], a paire,

To chuse of them which might content myne[51] eye;

But hir I sought, I could nowhere espie[52].

I spake them faire, and wisht them[53] well to fare—

"Yet[54] soe yt is, I must haue fresher ware;

Wherefore, dame Bawde, as daintie as you bee[55],

Fetch gentle mistris Francis forth to[56] me."

"By Halliedame[57]," quoth she, "and Gods oune mother,

I well perceaue you are a wylie[58] brother;

For if there be a morsell of more[59] price,

You'll smell it out, though I be nare so[60] nice.

As you desire, so shall you swiue with hir[61],

But think, your purse-strings shall abye-it deare[62];

For, he that will eate quailes must lauish crounes[63],

And Mistris Francis, in her veluett gounes[64],

And ruffs and perwigs as fresh as Maye[65],

Can not be kept with half a croune[66] a daye."

"Of price, good hostess[67], we will not debate,

Though[68] you assize me at the highest rate;

Onelie conduct me to this bonnie[69] bell.

And tenne good gobbs I will unto thee tell[70],

Of golde or siluer, which shall lyke thee[71] best,

So much doe I hir companie[72] request."

Awaie[73] she went: so sweete a thing is golde,

That (mauger) will inuade[74] the strongest holde.

"Hey-ho! she coms, that hath my hearte in keepe[75]

Sing Lullabie, my cares, and falle a-sleepe[76]."

Sweeping she coms[77], as she would brush the ground;

Hir ratling silkes my sences doe confound[78].

"Oh, I am rauisht: voide the chamber streight[79];

For I must neede's upon hir[80] with my weight."

"My Tomalin," quoth shee, and then she smilde[81].

"I, I," quoth I, "soe more men are beguild[82]

With smiles, with flatt'ring wordes, and fained cheere[83],

When in their deedes their falsehood doeth appeare[84]."

"As how, my lambkin," blushing, she replide[85],

"Because I in this dancing[86] schoole abide?

If that it be, that breede's this[87] discontent,

We will remoue the camp[88] incontinent:

For shelter onelie, sweete heart, came[89] I hither,

And to auoide the troblous stormie[90] weather;

But now the coaste is cleare, we will[91] be gonne,

Since, but thy self, true louer[92] I haue none."

With that she sprung full lightlie to my lips[93],

And fast about the neck me colle's, and clips[94];

She wanton faints[95], and falle's vpon hir bedd,

And often tosseth[96] too and fro hir head;

She shutts hir eyes[97], and waggles with her tongue:

"Oh, who is able to abstaine so long?[98]"

"I com! I com! sweete lyning be[99] thy leaue:"

Softlie my fingers up theis curtaine heaue[100],

And make me happie, stealing by degreese[101].

First bare hir leggs, then creepe up to hir kneese[102];

From thence ascend unto her mannely[103] thigh—

The Choise of Valentines - Or the Merie Ballad of Nash His Dildo

(A pox on lingring when I am so[104] nighe!).

Smock, climbe[105] a-pace, that I maie see my ioyes;

Oh heauen and paradize are all[106] but toyes

Compar'd with this sight I now[107] behould,

Which well might keepe a man from being olde.

A prettie rysing wombe without a weame[109],

That shone as bright as anie siluer streame[110];

And bare out like the bending of an[111] hill,

At whose decline a fountaine dwelleth still[112];

That hath his mouth besett with uglie bryers[113],

Resembling much a duskie nett of wyres[114];

A loftie buttock, barrd with azure veines[115],

Whose comelie swelling, when my hand distreines[116],

Or wanton checketh with a harmlesse stype[117],

It makes the fruites of loue oftsoone[118] be rype,

And pleasure pluckt too tymelie from the stemme[119]

To dye ere it hath seene Jerusalem[120].

O Gods! that euer anie thing so[121] sweete,

So suddenlie should fade awaie[122], and fleete!

Hir armes are spread, and I am all unarm'd[123],

Lyke one with Ouid's cursed hemlocke charm'd[124];

So are my Limms unwealdlie for the fight[125]

That spend their strength in thought of hir[126] delight.

What shall I doe to shewe my self a man?

It will not be for ought that beawtie can[128].

I kisse, I clap, I feele[129], I view at will,

Yett dead he lyes[130], not thinking good or ill.

"Unhappie me," quoth shee, "and wilt' not stand?[131]

Com, lett me rubb and chafe[132] it with my hand!

Perhaps the sillie worme is labour'd[133] sore,

And wearied that it can[134] doe noe more;

If it be so, as I am greate a-dread[135],

I wish tenne thousand times that I were[136] dead.

How ere it is, no meanes shall want[137] in me,

That maie auaile to his recouerie[138]."

Which saide, she tooke and rould it on hir thigh[139],

And when she look't on't, she would weepe and sighe;[140]

She dandled it, and dancet it up and doune[141],

Not ceasing till she rais'd it from his swoune[142].

And then he flue on hir as he[143] were wood,

And on hir breeche did hack and foyne[144] a-good;

He rub'd, and prickt, and pierst her[145] to the bones,

Digging as farre as eath[146] he might for stones;

Now high, now lowe, now stryking[147] shorte and thicke;

Now dyuing deepe, he toucht hir[148] to the quicke;

Now with a gird[149] he would his course rebate,

Straite would he take him to a statlie[150] gate;

Plaie while him list, and thrust he neare so[151] hard,

Poore pacient Grissill lyeth at hir warde[152],

And giue's, and takes, as blythe and free[153] as Maye,

And ere-more meete's him in the midle[154] waye.

On him hir eyes continualy[155] were fixt;

With hir eye-beames his melting looke's[156] were mixt,

Which, like the Sunne, that twixt two glasses plaies[157],

From one to th' other cast's rebounding[158] rayes.

He, lyke a starre that, to reguild[159] his beames

Sucks-in the influence of Phebus[160] streames,

Imbathes the lynes of his descending[161] light

In the bright fountaines of hir clearest sight[162].

She, faire as fairest Planet[163] in the skye,

Hir puritie[164] to noe man doeth denye;

The verie chamber that enclouds[165] her shine

Lookes lyke the pallace of that God deuine[166],

Who leades the daie about the Zodiake[167],

And euerie euen discends to th'oceane[168] lake;

So fierce and feruent is her radiance[169],

Such fyrie stakes she darts at euerie glance[170]

As might enflame the icie limmes[171] of age,

And make pale death his seignedrie to aswage;[172]

To stand and gaze upon her orient lamps[173],

Where Cupid all his chiefest ioyes encamps[174],

And sitts, and playes with euery atomie[175-6]

That in hir Sunne-beames swarme aboundantlie.

Thus gazing, and thus striuing, we perseuer[177]:

But what so firme that maie continue euer?[178]

"Oh not so fast," my rauisht Mistriss cryes[179],

"Leaste my content, that on[180] thy life relyes,

Be brought too-soone from his delightfull seate[181],

And me unwares of hoped bliss defeate[182].

Together lett us marche unto content[183],

And be consumed with one blandishment[184]."

As she prescrib'd so kept we crotchet-time[185],

And euerie stroake in ordre lyke a chyme[186],

Whilst she, that had preseru'd me by hir pittie[187],

Unto our musike fram'd a groaning dittie[188].

"Alass! alass! that loue should be a sinne!

Euen now my blisse and sorrowe doeth[190] beginne.

Hould wyde thy lapp, my louelie[191] Danae,

And entretaine the golden shoure so free[192],

That trikling falles[193] into thy treasurie.

As Aprill-drops not half so[194] pleasant be,

Nor Nilus overflowe to Ægipt plaines[195]

As this sweet-streames that all hir ioints imbaynes[196].

With "Oh!" and "Oh!" she itching moues hir hipps[197],

And to and fro full lightlie starts and skips[198]:

She ierkes hir leggs, and sprauleth[199] with hir heeles;

No tongue maie tell the solace[200] that she feeles,

"I faint! I yeald! Oh, death! rock me[201] a-sleepe!

Sleepe! sleepe desire! entombed[202] in the deepe!"

"Not so, my deare," my dearest saint[203] replyde,

"For, from us yett, thy spirit maie[204] not glide

Untill the sinnowie channels[205] of our blood

Without their source from this imprisoned[206] flood;

And then will we (that then will com too[207] soone),

Dissolued lye, as though our dayes were donne."

The whilst I speake, my soule is fleeting[209] hence,

And life forsakes his fleshie[210] residence.

Staie, staie sweete ioye, and leaue me not forlorne

Why shouldst thou fade that art but newelie borne?

"Staie but an houre, an houre[213] is not so much:

But half an houre; if that[214] thy haste is such,

Naie, but a quarter—I will aske no more—

That thy departure (which torments me sore),

Maie be alightned with a little pause[217],

And take awaie this passions sudden[218] cause."

He heare's me not; hard-harted as he is,

He is the sonne of Time, and hates my blisse.

Time nere looke's backe, the riuers nere returne;[221]

A second springe must help me or[222] I burne.

No, no, the well is drye that should refresh me[223],

The glasse is runne of all my destinie:

Nature of winter learneth nigardize

Who, as he ouer-beares the streame with ice

That man nor beaste maie of their pleasance taste,

So shutts she up hir conduit all in haste,

And will not let hir Nectar ouer-flowe,

Least mortall man immortall ioyes should knowe.

Adieu! unconstant loue, to thy disporte

Adieu! false mirth, and melodie too short;

Adieu! faint-hearted instrument of lust;

That falselie hath betrayde our equale trust.

Hence-forth no more will I implore thine[235] ayde,

Or thee, or man of cowardize upbrayde[236].

My little dilldo shall suply[237] their kinde:

A knaue, that moues[238] as light as leaues by winde;

That[239] bendeth not, nor fouldeth anie deale,

But stands as stiff as he were made of steele;

And playes at peacock twixt my leggs right blythe[241],

And doeth my tickling swage with manie a sighe.

For, by saint Runnion! he'le[243] refresh me well;

And neuer make my tender bellie[244] swell.

Poore Priapus! whose triumph now must falle[245],

Except thou thrust this weakeling to the walle[246].

Behould! how he usurps, in bed and bowre[247]

And undermines thy kingdom euerie howre;[248]

How slye he creepes betwixt[249] the barke and tree,

And sucks the sap, whilst sleepe detaineth[250] thee.

He is my Mistris page at euerie stound[251],

And soone will tent[252] a deepe intrenched wound.

He wayte's on Courtlie Nimphs that be so[253] coye,

And bids them skorne the blynd-alluring[254] boye.

He giues yong guirls their gamesome sustenance[255],

And euerie gaping mouth his full sufficeance.

He fortifies disdaine with forraine[257] artes,

And wanton-chaste deludes[258] all loving hartes.

If anie wight a cruell mistris serue's[259],

Or, in dispaire, (unhappie) pines and staru's[260],

Curse Eunuke dilldo, senceless counterfet[261]

Who sooth maie fill, but never can begett.

But, if revenge enraged with dispaire,

That such a dwarf his wellfare should empaire,

Would faine this womans secretarie[265] knowe,

Lett[266] him attend the markes that I shall showe:

He is a youth almost two handfulls highe[267],

Streight, round, and plumb, yett hauing[268] but one eye,

Wherein the rhewme so feruentlie doeth raigne[269],

That Stigian gulph maie scarce his teares containe;[270]

The Choise of Valentines - Or the Merie Ballad of Nash His Dildo

Attired in white veluet[271], or in silk,

And nourisht with whott water, or with milk[272],

Arm'd otherwhile[273] in thick congealed glasse,

When he, more glib, to hell be lowe[274] would passe.

Vpon a charriot of five wheeles he rydes[275],

The which an arme strong driuer stedfast[276] guides,

And often alters pace as wayes growe deepe,

(For who, in pathes unknowne[278], one gate can keepe?)

Sometimes he smoothlie slideth doune[279] the hill;

Another while[280], the stones his feete doe kill;

In clammie waies he treaddeth[281] by and by,

And plasheth and sprayeth all that be him nye[282].

So fares this iollie rider[283] in his race,

Plunging and sousing forward in lyke[284] case,

He dasht, and spurted, and he plodded[285] foule,

God giue thee shame, thou blinde[286] mischapen owle!

Fy-fy, for grief: a ladies chamberlaine[287],

And canst not thou thy tatling tongue refraine?[288]

I reade thee beardles blab[289], beware of stripes,

And be aduised what thou vainelie[290] pipes;

Thou wilt be whipt with nettles for this geare[291]

If Cicelie shewe but of thy knauerie[292] heere.

The Choise of Valentines - Or the Merie Ballad of Nash His Dildo

Saint Denis shield me from such female sprites!²⁹³

Regarde not, Dames, what Cupids Poete²⁹⁴ writes:

I pennd this storie onelie²⁹⁵ for my selfe,

Who, giuing suck unto a childish Elfe²⁹⁶,

And quitte discourag'd in my nurserie²⁹⁷,

Since all my store seemes to hir penurie²⁹⁸.

I am not as was Hercules the stout,

That to the seaventh iournie³⁰⁰ could hould out;

I want those hearbe's and rootes of Indian soile³⁰¹,

That strengthen wearie members in their toile³⁰²—

Druggs and Electuaries of new devise³⁰³,

Doe shunne my purse, that trembles at the price[304].

Sufficeth all I haue, I yeald hir hole[305]

Which, for a poore man, is a princelie dole,

I paie our hostess scott and lott at moste[307],

And looke as leane and lank as anie[308] ghoste;

What can[309] be added more to my renowne?

She lyeth breathlesse; I am taken doune;[310]

The waves doe swell, the tydes climbe or'e the banks;[311]

Judge, gentlemen! if I deserue not thanks?[312]

And so, good night! unto[313] you euer'ie one;

For loe, our thread is spunne, our plaie is donne[314].

Claudito iam vinos Priapa, sat prata biberunt [sic[a]].

Tho. Nash.

---

a   This does not scan; and, moreover, seems incorrectly transcribed, even making allowance for Nash's adaptation of a well-known line; *cf.* Virgil, *Eclogue* iii., line 111—"Claudite jam rivos, pueri, sat prata biberunt," "Now shut the hatches (in the banks of the stream), O lads, the pastures have drunk enough."

*T*hus* *hath my penne presum'd to please my friend—*

Oh mightst thou lykewise please Apollo's eye.

No, Honor brooke's no such impietie,

Yett Ouids wanton Muse did not offend.

He is the fountaine whence my streames doe flowe—

Forgive me if I speake as I was taught,

A lyke to women, utter all I knowe,

As longing to unlade so bad a fraught.

My mynde once purg'd of such lasciuious witt,

With purifide words and hallowed verse,

Thy praises in large volumes shall rehearce,

That better maie thy grauer view befitt.

Meanewhile yett rests, you smile at what I write;

Or, for attempting, banish me your sight.

Thomas Nash.

* Quite detached, on page 94 of the Rawl. MS. (the text commences on page 96), are a few lines entitled "The Epilogue," which are obviously part of the above, albeit more than usually imperfectly copied. Why so placed does not appear, especially as several blank pages immediately follow the conclusion of the Bodleian copy.

NOTES

1. Title, *The Choosing of Valentines*, Nashes Dildo.

2 *yong*, younge; *their iollie roguerie*, their brauery; *iollie*, Fr. *joli*, pretty, fine. *Bravery*, finery; *Cf.* Holinshed's *Chron. of Eng.*, 55—The ancient Britons painted their bodies "which they esteemed a great braverie."

3 *Rose earelie in the morne fore*, Rose in the morning before; *daie*, daye.

4 *soe trimme and gaie*, soe fresh and gaye.

5 *summer sheene*, somers shene.

6 *haidegaies on*, high degree in.

7 *alas at Easter, or*, allso at Ester and.

8 *Perambulate*, preambulate.

9 *to som*, into some; *abbordring*, bordering.

10 *taste the creame and cakes*, tast the cakes and creame.

11 *Or*, To.

12 *by Bachelrie of Maningtree*, by the bachelours of magnanimity. "Manningtree, in Essex, formerly enjoyed the privilege of fairs, by the tenure of exhibiting a certain number of stage plays yearly. It appears also, from other

The Choise of Valentines - Or the Merie Ballad of Nash His Dildo

intimations, that there were great festivities there, and much good eating, at Whitsun ales, and other times."— Nares.

13   *Where to, the contrie franklins*, Whether our Country Franklins.

14   *Jhon and Jone com*, John and Joane come.

15   *Euen*, Even; *hallowes*, Hallowes; *Saint*, Sainct.

16   *doeth*, doth; *louers*, lovers; *those*, omitted in Rawlinson.

17   *ladies*, Ladyes.

18   *she*, shee; *valentine*, valentyne.

19   *woe, alass*, out, alas.

20   *an upper*, another.

21   *-haft and crab-tree face*, with his crabbed face.

22   *scar'd hir*, scard her; *the*, that.

23   *And now she was compel'd for Sanctuarie*, And she, poore wench, compeld for Sanctuary.

24   *unto*, into; *venery*, Venery.

25   *bouldlie,*, bouldly; *enquire*, inquire.

26 *hackneis*, hackneyes. Hackney, a person or thing let out for promiscuous use, *e.g.*, a horse, a whore, a literary drudge. *Cf.* "The hobby-horse is but a colt, and your love perhaps a hackney."—*Love's Labour Lost*, iii., 1.

27 *crau'd*, craud.

29 *Therwith out stept*, With that, stept forth; *three chinnd*, three-chinde. Foggie = fat, bloated, having hanging flesh. *Cf.* "Some three chind foggie dame."—Dolarney, *Primrose*.

30 *us'd*, vsd; *yong*, younge.

31 *ask't*, askt; *I ment as I profest*, soothe were my request.

32 *onelie ask't*, onely moud.

33 *it*, yt.

34 *com*, come; *give*, giue; *Jill*, Gill.

35 *"Why, Sir."* quoth shee, *"if that be your demande,* "If that yt be," quoth she, "that you demaunde."

36 *Com laye me a God's-pennie*, then giue me first a godes peny. "God's-pennie, an earnest-pennie."—Florio, p. 36.

37 *oratorie siccarlie*, oratory, siccarly. "Oratory," properly a private chapel or closet for prayer; here a

canting term for brothel: cf. abbess = bawd; nun = whore, and so forth. "Siccarly," certainly, surely "Thou art here, sykerlye, Thys churche to robb with felonye," MS. Cantab Ff. ii., 38, f. 240.

38   *heere*, in; *nicarie*, deuory. "Nick," female *pudendum*: hence nickery, copulation. Deuory may either be Fr. *devoir*, duty; or devoure, to ravish, to deflower.

39   *offertorie*, affidavit.

40   *wee'le*, Ile.

41   *hearing hir so ernest*, seeing her soe earnest.

42   *Gave hir hir*, I gaue her her; *and she the dore unlocks*, and she the doare vnlockes.

43   *In am I entered*, Nowe I am entered; *venus*, sweet Venus.

44   *where's this female*, where's the female; *do this*, do the.

45   *By*, through; *meanders and by crankled*, meander and through crooked.

46   *Shee leades*, Shee leads; *Aucthor saies*, author sayes.

47   *we came within*, I came vnto; *shadie*, shady.

48 *bounsing vestalls*, bouncing vestures; *skirmish*, skyrmish; *oft*, omitted.

49 *shee*, she; *leather chaire*, Lether chayre.

50 *prettie Trulls*, wenches straight.

51 *To chuse of them*, And bad me choose; *myne*, my.

52 *hir*, she; *no where espie*, noe waye espye.

53 *them*, her; *them* her.

54 *Yet*, But.

55 *Bawde*, baud; *as daintie*, soe dainty; *bee*, be.

56 *forth to*, vnto.

57 *Halliedame*, Holy Dame; *she*, shee; *Gods oune*, gods one.

58 *wylie*, wyly.

59 *more*, better.

60 *You'l smell*, youle find; *nare so*, now soe.

61 *hir*, her.

62 *think*, look; *purse-strings*, purse-stringes; *abye it deare*, abide yt deere.

63 *that will eate quailes*, whoole feed on quayles; *crounes*, crownes.

64 *Mistris Francis*, Mistres Fraunces; *veluett gounes*, velvett gownes.

65 *And ruffs*, Her ruffe; *perwigs*, perriwigge; *as*, soe; *Maye*, May.

66 *with half a croune*, for half a crowne.

67 *hostess*, hostes; *we*, wee.

68 *Though*, although.

69 *bonnie*, bonny.

70 *tenne*, tenn; *gobbs I will unto thee tell*, goblets vnto thee Ile tell. "Gob, a portion" (H).

71 *lyke thee*, like you.

72 *doe I hir companie*, I doe her company.

73 *Awaie*, Awaye; *thing*, worde.

74 *That (mauger) will inuade*, it makes invasion in.

75 *Hey-ho*, Loe! here; *hearte*, harte; *keepe*, keeping.

76 *Lullabie*, lullaby; *and falle a sleepe*, fall a sleeping.

77 *coms*, comes; *ground*, ground.

78 *Hir*, her; *silkes*, silcke; *confound*, Confound.

79 *Oh*, Awaye; *rauisht*, ravisht; *voide*, voyd; *chamber*, Chamber; *streight*, straight.

80 *For I must neede's be on hir*, I must be straight vppon her.

81 *smilde*, smiled.

82 *beguilde*, beguiled.

83 *With smiles, with flatt'ring wordes, and fained cheere*, With sighes and flattering woordes and teares.

84 *their*, your; *their*, much; *doeth appeare*, still apeares.

85 *how*, How; *lambkin*, Tomalyn; *replide*, replied.

86 *dancing*, dauncing.

87 *it be*, be it; *this*, thy.

88 *camp*, campe.

89 *onelie*, only; *sweete heart*, sweete harte; *came*, cam.

90 *auoide*, avoyd; *troblous and stormie*, troublesome, stormye.

91 *But now,* And since; *coaste,* coast; *we wil,* I will.

92 *Since,* for; *louer,* louers.

93 *sprung,* sprunge; *lips,* lippes.

94 *And fast about the neck me colle's and clips,* and about my neck she hugges, she calles, she clippes. "Coll or "cull," to kiss, to embrace; so also "clip."

95 *faints,* faynes; *vpon hir,* vppon the.

96 *tosseth,* tosses; *and fro hir,* and froe her.

97 *shutts hir eyes,* shakes her feete.

98 *who,* whoe; *abstaine,* forbeare; *long,* longe.

99 *I com, I com,* I come, I come; *lyning,* Ladye; *be,* by.

100 *Softlie my fingers up this curtaine heaue,* softly my curtaines lett my fingers heaue.

101 *make,* send; *happie,* happye; *stealing,* sailing; *degreese,* degrees.

102 *First bare hir leggs, then creepe up to hir kneese,* First vnto the feete, and then vnto the kneese.

103 *From thence,* And soe; *unto,* vnto; *mannely,* manly.

104 *lingring,* lingering; *am so,* come soe.

105 *Smock*, Smocke; *climbe*, clime.

106 *Oh heaven and paradise are all*, all earthly pleasures seeme to this.

107 *Compar'd with this sight I now*, Compard be these delightes which I.

109 *prettie rysing*, prettye rising; *weame*, wenne. "Wem," spot or blemish.

110 *shone*, shine(s); *anie siluer streame*, any christall gemme.

111 *bare*, beares; *bending*, riseing; *an*, a.

112 *a fountaine dwelleth still*, the(r) runnes a fountayne still.

113 *his*, her; *uglie bryers*, rugged briers.

114 *duskie*, duskye; *wyres*, wires.

115 *loftie*, lusty; *veines*, vaines.

116 *comelie*, comely; *distreines*, restraines. "Distreines," to seize, to touch.

117 *wanton*, harmles; *harmlesse stype*, wanton gripe.

118 *fruites of loue oftsoone*, fruite thereof too soone

119 *And*, A; *too tymelie*, to tymely; *the stemme*, his springe.

120 *To dye ere it hath seene Jerusalem*, it is, dyes ere it can enioye the vsed thinge.

121 *Gods*, Godes; *euer anie*, ever any; *so*, soe.

122 *So suddenlie*, soe suddenly; *awaie*, awaye.

123 *Hir*, Her; *are spread and I am all unarm'd*, and legges and all were spredd, But I was all vnarmed.

124 *Lyke*, like; *with*, that; *charm'd*, charmd.

125 Omitted in Rawl. MS.

126 *spend their*, spent there; *hir*, your.

128 *It*, Yt; *beawtie cann*, beauty can.

129 *clap*, clipp; *I feele, I view*, I wincke, I feele.

130 *dead he lyes*, lyes he dead; *thinking*, feeling.

131 *Unhappie me*, By Holly dame; *stand*, staund.

132 *Com*, now; *rubb*, roule; *chafe*, rub; *with*, in.

133 *Perhaps*, perhapps; *sillie*, seely; *is labour'd*, hath laboured.

134 *wearied that it can*, worked soe that it cann.

135 *If it be so*, Which if it be; *am greate a-dread*, doe greately dread.

136 *tenne*, ten; *were*, weare.

137 *How ere it is*, What ere it be; *no*, noe; *want*, lacke.

138 *maie auaile to*, maye avayle for; *recouerie*, recoverye.

139 *saide*, said; *and rould*, & rowld; *hir thigh*, her thighe.

140 *And when she look't on't she would weepe and sighe*, and looking downe on it, did groane and sighe.

141 *dandled*, haundled; *dancet*, daunced; *up*, vpp; *doune*, downe.

142 *she rais'd*, shee raisd; *his swoune*, her sound.

143 *he flue*, it flewe; *hir*, her; *he*, it.

144 *hir breeche did hack and fayne*, her breech laboured & foam'd.

145 *prickt, and pierst her*, peirct her euer.

146 *farre*, deepe; *might*, could digg; "eath," easy.

147 *stryking*, stricking; *and*, &.

The Choise of Valentines - Or the Merie Ballad of Nash His Dildo

148 *Now dyuing deepe he toucht hir,* And diving deeper, peircte her.

149 *gird,* girde.

150 *Straite,* then; *statlie,* stately.

151 *him,* he; *so,* soe.

152 *pacient Grissill,* patient Grissell; *hir warde,* his ward.

153 *blythe,* blith; *free,* fresh.

154 *ere-more,* euer; *midle,* middle of the.

155 *him hir eyes continualy,* her his eyes Continually.

156 *hir eye-beames his,* his eye-browes her; *looke's,* eyes.

157 *twixt,* betwixt; *plaies,* playes.

158 *one,* the one; *th'other cast's rebounding,* the other casting redounding.

159 *He lyke,* She like; *reguild,* requite.

160 *Sucks-in,* suckes; *of Phebus,* of sweete Phebus.

161 *lynes,* beames: *descending,* discinding.

162 *bright,* deepest; *hir dearest sight,* the purest light.

163   *Planet*, plannet.

164   *Hir puritie*, her puritye.

165   *verie chamber*, verye Chamber; *enclouds*, includes.

166   *Lookes lyke*, seemes as; *that God deuine*, the gods devine.

167   *Who*, Whoe; *daie*, daye; *Zodiake*, Zodiacke.

168   *euerie euen discends to th'oceane*, in the even, settes of the ocean.

169   *So fierce*, soe feirce; *is hir radiance*, in her radiaunce.

170   *fyrie stakes*, flyeing breath; *darts*, dartes; *euerie glance*, every glaunce.

171   *enflame*, inflame; *icie limmes*, verry mappe.

172   *make*, cause; *his seignedrie to aswage*, him suddenly tasswage.

173   *To*, and; *upon her*, vppon those; *lamps*, lampes.

174   *his chiefest ioyes encamps*, his ioyes incampes.

175-6   Omitted in Rawl. MS.

177   *Thus gazing, and thus striuing, we perseuer*, Thus striking, thus gazeing, we perseuere.

178   *what so firme*, nought soe sure; *maie*, will; *euer*, ever.

179   *Oh!* Fleete; *rauisht Mistris cryes*, ravisht senses cries.

180   *Leaste*, sith; *content that on*, Content vppon.

181   *Be*, Which; *too*, soe; *seat*, seates.

182   *And me unwares of hoped bliss defeat*, me vnawares of blissefull hope defeates. Here occur two lines in the Rawl. MS. which do not appear in the Petyt MS., as follows:

Togeather lett our equall motions stirr,

Togeather lett vs liue and dye, my deare;

183   *Together lett us marche unto content*, Togeather let vs march with one contente.

184   *consumed with one blandishment*, Consum(e)d without languishmente.

185   *prescrib'd, so kept we crochet*, prescribed so keepe we clocke and.

186   *lyke*, like; *chyme*, chime.

187   *Whilst she*, soe shee; *had preseru'd*, here preferd; *pittie*, pittye.

The Choise of Valentines - Or the Merie Ballad of Nash His Dildo

188   *Unto*, vnto; *musike*, musicke; *dittie*, dittye.

190   *Euen*, even; *blisse and sorrowe doeth*, ioyes and sorrowes doe.

191   *lapp*, lappe; *louelie*, louely.

192   *entretaine the*, entertaine this; *shoure so free*, showry see.

193   *trikling falles*, drisling fall(es); *treasurie*, treasurye.

194   *As Aprill-drops*, Sweete Aprill flowers; *half so*, halfe soe.

195   *overflowe to Ægipt-plaines*, overfloweinge Egipt playne.

196   *As this sweet-streames*, as is the balme; *hir ioints imbaynes*, her woombe destreynes.

197   *With Oh! and Oh! she itching moues hir hipps*, Now! oh now! she trickling moues her lippes.

198   *And*, and often; *full lightlie starts and skips*, she lightly startes and skippes.

199   *ierkes*, yerkes; *leggs*, legges; *sprauleth*, fresketh.

200   *No*, noe; *maie*, can; *solace*, pleasures.

201 *I faint! I yeald! Oh death, rock me*, I come! I come! sweete death, rocke mee.

202 *entombed*, intombe me.

203 *my deare, my dearest saint*, my deare, and dearest she.

204 *For, from us yett, thy spirit maie*, from us two (yett) this pleasure must.

205 *Untill*, Vntill; *channels*, Chambers.

206 *Without their source*, Withould themselues; *imprisoned*, newe prisoned.

207 *will we*, we will; *com too*, come soe.

209 *whilst*, whilest; *speake*, speke; *is fleeting*, in stealing.

210 *fleshie*, earthly.

213 *but an houre*, but one houre; *an houre is*, one houre is; *so*, soe

214 *But*, nay; *if that*, and if.

217 *Maie be alightned with a little pause*, Maye now be lengthened by a litle pawse.

218 *awaie*, awaye; *sudden*, suddaine.

221 *riuers nere returne*, riuer nere returnes.

222 *springe*, spring; *must helpe me or*, must helpe, or elles.

223-34 Omitted in Rawl. MS.

235 *Hence-forth no more will I implore thine*, Hensforth I will noe more implore thine.

236 *or man of cowardize upbrayde*, for ever of Cowardise shall vpprayd.

237 *dilldo*, dildoe; *suply their*, supplye your.

238 *knaue*, youth; *moues*, is; *by*, in.

239 *That*, He; *anie*, any.

241-42 Omitted in Rawl. MS.

243 *For, by saint Runnion, he'le*, And when I will he doth.

244 *make*, makes; *bellie*, belly.

245 *whose triumph now*, thy kingdome needes; *falle*, fall.

246 *Except*, eccept; *walle*, wall.

247 *usurps*, vsurpes; *boure*, bower.

The Choise of Valentines - Or the Merie Ballad of Nash His Dildo

248 *undermines*, vndermines; *euerie howre*, euery hower.

249 *sly he*, slyly; *betwixt*, betwene.

250 *sucks*, suckes; *whilst*, while; *detaineth*, deteyneth.

251 *page*, lake; *stound*, sound. "Stound," a moment.

252 "tent," to search out.

253 *Courtlie Nimphs*, courtly nimphs; *be so*, are full.

254 *blynd-alluring*, blind-alluring.

255-6 Omitted in Rawl. MS.

257 *fortifies disdaine*, fortifyes disdayne; *forraine*, foraigne.

258 *And wanton-chaste deludes*, while wantons chast delude.

259 *anie*, any; *Mistris serue's*, Mistres serue.

260 *Or*, and; *(unhappie) pines and staru's*, full deeply pyne and sterue.

261-64 Omitted in Rawl. MS.

265 *womans secretarie*, woemans secretary.

266 *Lett*, let.

267 *handfulls highe*, handfulles high.

268 *plumb*, plump; *yett hauing*, and having.

269 *rhewme so feruentlie doeth raigne*, rheume soe fervently doth raine.

270 *That*, the; *gulph maie*, gulfe can; *containe*, conteyne. Here follow, in the Rawl. MS., lines 290-93 of the Petyt; lines 292-3 being also reversed in the Rawl. text.

271 *Attired*, attird; *veluet*, velvet.

272 *nourisht*, norisht; *hott*, warme; *milk*, milke. "Whott," hot.

273 *Arm'd otherwhile*, Running sometymes.

274 *more glib*, more like; *to hell be lowe*, downe into hell.

275 *charriot*, chariot; *rydes*, rides.

276 *The which an arme strong driuer stedfast*, An arme strong guider steadfastly him.

278 *who*, whoe; *pathes unknowne*, places vnknowne; *gate*, pace.

279 *Sometimes*, sometymes; *smoothlie slideth doune a*, smoothly slippeth downe a.

280 *Another while*, some other tymes.

281 *clammie waies*, clayey wayes; *treaddeth*, treadeth.

282 *plasheth and sprayeth*, placeth himself &; *be him nye*, standeth by.

283 *So*, soe; *iollie rider*, royall rider.

284 *Plunging and sousing*, Plungeing & sowsing; *lyke*, like.

285 *He dasht, and spurted, and he plodded*, Bedasht, bespotted, and beplotted.

286 *blinde*, foule.

287 *Fy-fy, for grief*, But free from greife; *ladies chamberlaine*, ladyes chamberlayne.

288 *not thou*, thou not: *refraine*, refrayne.

289 *reade thee*, tell the; *blab*, blabb. "Reade," warn.

290 *aduised*, advisd; *thou vainelie*, thou soe vainely.

291 Transposed in Rawl. MS. with line 292; *wilt*, shouldst.

292 *Cicelie shewe but*, Illian queene knowe; *knauerie*, bravery.

The Choise of Valentines - Or the Merie Ballad of Nash His Dildo

293 *Denis shield*, Dennis sheild; *female sprites*, femall sprightes.

294 *Dames*, dames; *Cupid's Poet*, Cupid's poett.

295 *pennd*, pen; *storie onelie*, story onely.

296 *Who giuing suck unto a childish Elfe*, And, giving yt to such an actuall Elfe.

297 *And*, am; *discourag'd*, discoraged; *nurserie*, mistery.

298 *hir*, her; *penurie*, misery.

300 *seaventh iournie*, seauenth Iourny.

301 *want*, wantes; *hearbe's*, omitted; *and*, &; *soile*, soyle.

302 *wearie*, weary; *toile*, toyle.

303 *Druggs or Electuaries of new devise*, Or drugges or electuaryes of newe devises.

304 *Doe shunne*, that shame; *that trembles*, & tremble; *the*, thie; *price*, prices. In the Rawl. MS., lines 307-8 of the Petyt MS. follow here.

305 *Sufficeth all I haue, I yeald hir hole*, For that I allwayes had, I payd the wole.

307 *I paie our hostess*, I paid of both the; *and*, &; *at moste*, allmost.

73

308 *And,* yet; *and,* &; *anie,* any.

309 *can,* cann.

310 *doune,* downe.

311 *climbe,* clims; *banks,* bankes.

312 *gentlemen, if I,* gentleweomen doth this; *not thanks,* no thankes.

313 *so,* soe: *unto,* vnto.

314 *thread,* thred; *plaie is donne,* playes done.

www.ingramcontent.com/pod-product-compliance
Lightning Source LLC
Chambersburg PA
CBHW022120090426
42743CB00008B/941